I0568514

Dating

Advice

Learn the Essentials on How to Date, Approach and Talk

(Attract and Get a Girlfriend or Boyfriend by Seducing)

Billy Scott

Published By **Tyson Maxwell**

Billy Scott

All Rights Reserved

*Dating Advice: Learn the Essentials on How to Date,
Approach and Talk (Attract and Get a Girlfriend or
Boyfriend by Seducing)*

ISBN 978-1-998769-39-1

No part of this guidebook shall be reproduced in any form without permission in writing from the publisher except in the case of brief quotations embodied in critical articles or reviews.

Legal & Disclaimer

The information contained in this ebook is not designed to replace or take the place of any form of medicine or professional medical advice. The information in this ebook has been provided for educational & entertainment purposes only.

The information contained in this book has been compiled from sources deemed reliable, and it is accurate to the best of the Author's knowledge; however, the Author cannot guarantee its accuracy and validity and cannot be held liable for any errors or omissions. Changes are periodically made to this book. You must consult your doctor or get professional medical advice before using any of the suggested remedies, techniques, or information in this book.

Table Of Contents

Introduction

While most people love dating, it's not something they should be doing. People created children thousands of years ago through their survival skills. People with something were the only ones who could survive. They pass that something on to their children, to their grandchildren and to their great-grandchildren.

Procreating is now a common goal. Humans no longer have to fight for survival. This is a great thing. Men lost sight of what it meant to be a man over time.

This is both tragic and the reason so many marriages fall apart.

I am sure you have heard of the couple that were so happy in the beginning but who eventually stopped loving each other.

It's a very common phenomenon, which makes it sad. Why?

Why are so many people in love but cannot stand each other over time? Is it time?

The price of a relationship is not the most important thing. However, it does not mean that time is not an agent. It's the same here. If you don't have a relationship with someone, then time will begin to take control and... eventually destroy them.

It is difficult to imagine how so many people can love one another so much, but still be apart.

It's because they love the impression others give them. Today, people are less real than the brands they see. At first, they try their best to make their date love them. But after a while, the act becomes repetitive and boring.

People discover that they are more successful apart. Some people are able to have kids or marry before realizing it. It is likely that the kids will make the same mistakes their parents did, and it will set them up for failure.

Now you can see why many people lose sight on what a real male looks like. A man of integrity is honest and true. A person of integrity.

This book is meant to do exactly that. I'll show you in the next chapters the exact steps to follow to become a charming and interesting person.

Chapter 1: What's Stopping You From Scoring With A Woman?

"Every chapter will bring with it new problems."

- Anonymous

There are many issues that come with dating. Many men will agree that your age plays an important role in finding the right partner, or winning the heart and affection of the woman you've been longing for. No matter what age group you fall into, dating is not easy. The way people view you in your 20s is very different from when you are 30.

You don't know why dating in your 20s is so difficult. It's your first graduation, so you don't know what the future holds. What is the point?

Society has made young people afraid to catch feelings. That's science. Jean Twenge from San Diego State University is a psychologist who studies generational differences. She claims that Gen Z, whom she calls iGen and which takes longer to become a person, means they take longer to date. Instead, they chose to use their 20s in order to explore their careers, their world, and their personal lives.

Dating issues when you are older than 30

You will learn new nuances as you navigate your new decade. Do not think you are good at dating after your 20s.

You might feel overwhelmed and frustrated again. You're not alone in feeling frustrated and overwhelmed when you start dating in your 30s.

The playing field has changed significantly, it is more narrow, and you will probably have more baggage now that you did in your 20s. There are two options. One, you can have your heart broken by someone else, and then there is the possibility that you will be dedicated to a job that takes up a lot more of your time. The pressure to be together is greater for you if you have fewer close friends.

Don't panic if this is your first time being single, or you just turned 30, and are starting to notice the changes in your daily life. This book will help guide you through the dating process, saving your love life. It doesn't matter how long you've been dating for more than twenty-five years and still haven't found your woman of choice.

What is stopping you from seeking out the woman who gets your blood pumping in your 40s and 30s?

* Age

I assume you will ask yourself this question when you first start dating in your 40s or 30s. It is about the difference in age between you and your woman of interest.

But is age really important? I'd say no. Don't let women get cut off because they are too young. Relationships are built on the love between two people. They support each other and have a great experience together, regardless of how far apart they are in age. Age differences might not matter as much as other considerations such as physical attraction and compatibility when two people meet up on a date.

* Past Experience

One reason many people end up single in their 30s, is because they've experienced heartbreak. You can blame it on ghosting, cheating and/or a breakup.

Single men over 30 should be happy that the past is gone. Let the bygones go. You don't want to be on the third date with your ex. Let it go! We all have skeletons within our closets. But that doesn't necessarily mean you have it to put on every day.

Although your past has shaped who you are today it is time to accept that your future is not based on your past. Instead, you should be focusing on where you stand now. Seek out the person in front you to see what life has for you.

* A Blurred Mindset

You may have dreamed of a girl, in your 20s, who would be able to drive a nice car and afford expensive restaurants. These are great things, but once you get into your 30s, these things will no longer be important to you.

Now is the time to start thinking about what you really want in a woman.

Start by writing down the names for the women you've dated. Next, list the top 5 most enjoyable things about them. Then, list them along with the top 5 least favorite things. You will probably see a pattern in your list. These positive qualities are what you should look out for in the girl that you choose to meet. This little exercise will help clear any confusion.

* High Expectations

Avoid settling for a partner that you don't feel will be around for long. This relationship will not be healthy and it will not last. But waiting for the perfect woman is not the best option. Accept this and be willing to make compromises. Welcome to an adult relationship.

The Mistakes Men Make When Dating Women

When it comes to relationships, we are all afraid of making errors. Your actions are what will define your relationship's future. One perfect move can make your life partner, while one mistake can send you into oblivion. How can you find out if you are making mistakes? This list will help you to determine whether or not you are making any mistakes. This will help determine if the path you are following is right for you.

* Acting as a Child

As children, our mom would hold our hands and lead us around. She would tell us what we should do and where to go. This shows us that we are used in letting a woman guide us.

You shouldn't do it with a woman you like. Women love men who have the ability to lead and are able to make decisions. You will always find a charm in bold and daring choices. Each time SHE chooses the restaurant or movie for the two of them, a small part of her attraction to you ceases. She will soon feel more like your mother than your girlfriend.

Consider this: If you don't have the ability to pick a restaurant, how can you make important decisions about your life? You have to make decisions about when you want to settle down, how to have a child, and when you want to leave. Stop being a child and start acting up.

* Never be impatient

Be patient and open to the possibility of a woman in her thirties deciding to date you. There is a good chance that you will lose her interest if your enthusiasm or pushing too hard are excessive. People who have experienced the impulsiveness of their 20s need to take time to get used the language and understand love. If you push your feelings on her, she might become suffocated and stop being able to breathe. Give her room to fall in your arms. Let her know that you are interested in her but don't insist on coming to her door every single day.

* Overthinking

Waiting for her is fine, but doing nothing is better than waiting for a miracle. Let's say you like a girl. You spend months looking into her, making a list her likes and dislikes and planning the perfect way to ask for her hand. Finally, the day arrives, and just a few moments before you make your move, a stranger approaches her and asks if she is interested in dating him. They start to talk about getting married and they continue to hang out together for many months. Every day you return home, weeping about it.

90% of dating comes down to taking the right actions at the right time.

We all know what happens. A man may see a woman that he likes but does not do anything because he is thinking about the consequences. He isn't going to make the same mistakes as he did in the past. He wants to be the one to convince her to love him. He might be trying to compose the perfect text while he holds his phone. The wrong type of action is to not take action. It is the wrong type.

* Thinking they can buy her love

Imagine that you have a job which pays well. Many men in their 40s, 30s, and 40s have it. You have money, the appearance, and everything a woman can desire. You meet a beautiful woman and you decide to go out. There is nothing wrong with going out with a woman to dinner. Both you and your partner are enjoying each other's company.

Things begin to turn sour when a guy starts to think he can make women love him or get attracted to his manhood by buying her stuff, such as drinks, expensive meals, rent payments, and so on. You shouldn't neglect your woman. Some women may even enjoy the surprise and extra care. Keep in mind, however, that women today have the ability to earn their own income. They don't need men to pay for everything. This leads to the 21st Century women realizing that men think they own them.

Modern women don't need men who can afford to buy them food and drinks. This would have been a wonderful gesture in the past. But what women really want is a man who will make them feel secure, respect their choices, and be able to support their decisions.

Make the right move

The next step after you've covered the main do's & don'ts in regards to how to behave and what to expect from a mature, adult relationship is to understand the importance of approaching women correctly.

Nowadays, you can spend more time on your phone or laptop than talking to someone in person. It is therefore outdated to worry about approaching women. There are many ways you can meet women. The greatest benefit of modern technology is this: you can get to know women in many different ways. But, women can have successful relationships if you show your strength, reach out to her and start a conversation.

It's still the main way to form relationships of any type, whether personal, professional or friendly. Even if you find a woman online, you'll eventually want to meet her face-to-face. That's how it gets going. It's a great way to make a first impression and seal the deal. It's a much better way to start the process.

Being calm and confident when speaking with women is a wonderful and innovative skill that will impress them greatly. It's possible to make connections with women you don't know. You can also let go of your nerves. Once you've made the right decision, it becomes much easier to make women feel attracted to you.

Chapter 2: Stop Neediness

As we know, the majority of society's needy are those who live in poverty. I am sure you are familiar with at least one. A nice man is someone who offers to help even if it's not asked. They will cancel the plan for you, will lie so that you don't get offended, some will make 2 people hate one another so they don't hate each other.

Most nice guys aren't really nice. They will do anything for you in order to get you to like them back. And if you don't, well, they will blame the other person.

"Ughhhh, I did so much and she doesn't even like it!"

"Ughhh! I told her that I was not like the other guys, and she finds excuses not dating me"

"She is such and b, she chose this guy just because it is younger, I'm done dealing with 7 graders."

While the last one was a joke it was true that most nice men fail to recognize that their lack in confidence and self-esteem is what makes them attractive. Confident people won't take responsibility for others' failures, and they don't waste any time trying to make them like themselves.

They will often make an apology, even when they are not responsible. They will do their best to keep the water at the right temperature and panic if they get into a dispute.

A confident man will tell his tale, acknowledge the things he does not like and then let the world know that he is not perfect. A confident man will never waste his time with people who won't make it happy. I'm not talking here about temporary happiness like sex and kissing. Real happiness is when someone makes you smile or you both have the ability to solve most of your problems together. The most important thing is to find someone who will make you feel happy and accept you for you are. If you like, make this a selection method.

You should think about people you have known for at minimum 2 or 3 months. Do you find yourself in the same situation as them? Are you worried that they will criticize you if you are honest with them? If you answer yes to the first, then those people may not be right for you. You may also be responsible. Because an honest and truthful person cannot pretend to being someone else.

You see, I only gave you a small piece of the picture. To stop becoming dependent around others, you need to tell the truth. I can show you some examples of fairly honest people who tell most truths, but end up with very few girls.

Think about the people who beg girls for dates. They may spend hours calling, texting, and even stalking girls, telling their love and how smart and beautiful they are. It is easy to see they are truthful. They will tell you the truth, but they can still be needy.

Their problems are not their words, but their intentions. It's almost like giving a girl a fake compliment, and then wondering why they don't understand it. Yes, the words were nice. But maybe you just wanted to have a conversation with them to get to to know them better. While that's fine, it's not the problem. Instead of saying "Hello. I want to get to know you", you gave her an insult that she doesn't understand.

It is obvious that girls speak a different tongue than men. We focus on words. If we tell someone that his hair is bad, then it is probably bad. However, if a girl does the same thing to another girl, he may not like it. So, she might tell him that her hair is awful to make her feel uncomfortable.

Girls language is like code language. Just learn to decode. You will need to think before your speak. This is vital. The next time you make a compliment, or offer any other type of compliment, you should ask yourself whether you are saying it to get something in return. It will make a big difference.

A confident man will not give a compliment in order to please a girl. A confident person says what he thinks, and believes what he says!

To get rid of his neediness, it is important for a man that he starts to value his own self. It is also known as self-esteem.

You need to be able to recognize your strengths and make improvements every day. And most importantly, you have the ability to change your thinking. Numerous studies have shown us that our thoughts can control our lives. You will think you're poor if you do. If you believe that you are stupid, then you'll grow up to be one. You'll attract the people you don't like, those who aren't worthy of respect. People who don't respect you, or treat you badly, will make you feel that you aren't worthy of more.

Who decides? Who gets the right to say "That's all that I deserve"? Nobody, except you, can tell you that you're an extraordinary trust and respect-worthy human being.

I learned how to respect myself and stand up for my rights through practice.

The next chapters will help you become less needy and more confident. If I give you the guidance and you learn the lessons, then you're well on your path to a healthy and happy relationship.

Chapter 3: Approaching A Woman

You are confident and well-dressed. You're at a bar when you spot the most attractive woman. How should you approach her? What will you say?

Keep in mind that you will always choose the most attractive woman around. Do not settle for a woman who is "too beautiful for you". This is a big no-no. Be the cool guy that your are. Never settle for less than the best.

It is a good idea to approach her and have a conversation. There is a way you can start a conversation that will be successful and get that woman's attention. The system is simple and straightforward. As we have already explained, our first impressions of someone are crucial because it is how we as humans form an opinion about them. In order to make her feel more comfortable, give her a peek into your personal life. It's a three-step process: make a comment about something you notice in your environment; then, share a bit of your life with her; then, ask a question. While it may sound complicated, this is actually quite simple to perform. Here's a good example:

(In a pub)

Me: How amusing that there are tennis rackets hung on the wall.

Woman: That is quite odd.

Me: It's like the tennis tournament last weekend, when I reached my finals. I made it to the finals, but was not victorious. I had a fantastic barbecue with my friends to celebrate.

Woman: Do you play tennis and have reached the finals of the game? You must be very good at it.

Me: Yes, that is what I do. It's one of the many hobbies I have. Is there any other sport you enjoy?

In the first sentence, I make a comment regarding something smart. However, she doesn't seem to be interested. I bring out my love of tennis. She seems a bit intrigued. Finally, I ask about her sports. The conversation continues and is very easy to keep going. You can be sure that some women will not respond or will not be interested. These women will not respond even if you use a Zeus-written pickup line. When you have gained her interest and want to end the conversation, tell your woman that you have a place to go. You could say, "Excuse moi, but it's time to leave. I'm hosting a party at my friend's place." You will need her number, however.

This is not a 100% guarantee. You might find that some women are in a very difficult mood, or they have something else going on. You might be rejected occasionally, and that's OK. Do not take rejections personal. You will begin to think negatively, which will affect your confidence and mental health. It's better than failing to try and fail than not trying at all. Don't give up on the chance to attract women by not trying. Rejections shouldn't cause you to panic. Remember that you are a confident, successful, cool person. You don't have to dwell on why this woman rejected your application. Never forget that failure is part the learning curve. Even if the first attempt fails, the second one will prove to be a better success. Consider this: if you continue to approach women and use this method for talking, you will be more successful with the 10th one than the 1st. What's the worst thing that can happen to you? You must make it a big deal.

Chapter 4: Let Her Live A Fantasy And Play With You As If It Were A Game

Questions that are asked during a game or test will be accepted.

They will be shocked if you ask them "Have ye ever had sex on a beach?" It will make you look like a pervert, if you ask them the question in a game that aims to ask embarrassing questions. She will then answer calmly.

You can't play tests or games with the entire date. Instead, all you can do is use your imagination to get your date into a Role Play.

Role Play allows you to express yourself freely. There are no restrictions or judgments. If you allow your daughter to play in a Roleplay Game that she finds spoiled and rebellious, you can also give her a spanking.

Role Play involves you and your partner in creating a dynamic story. You choose what to do, and what MAKE HER DO for the entire story. You control the story; you are the author.

Make sure she sees all the scenes you describe. Use cliches and talk about emotions.

For the human brain, the emotions created by imagination are just as real as those generated by actual events. If you have ever had a nightmare or experienced something frightening, it is likely that you fear. In reality, you will wake up shaking, sweaty, and confused. IDEM is used in a positive light. Imagine "talking to" a beautiful woman. It's real!

It is impossible to imagine a scene in the head when you describe something in words. The landscapes and faces of the protagonists are what you see when you read a novel. When I say to you to notice the font, it was because I used to write these words and then not to picture a beach with two elephants drinking champagne while watching sunset. By the time you hear my command, you will already have the command executed and can imagine what I want you to envision.

Role playing games can be extremely powerful. You will not understand what I am talking about if it isn't done. However, it is more difficult than actually doing it. I'll show you many more examples than those found on the pages before, and I'll also give you different scenarios.

You will always find points in every Role Game.

* You are doing something together

* It is you, the director of it all, who decides what she should do and what she should do.

* You hold a dominant, significant or powerful position

* she does something embarrassing or belittling

* photo of you having sex or any other intimate situation

Ideas for possible scenarios:

* A little girl or mischievous daughters that you must scold

* Lovers who have a prohibited relationship and run away together

* Ex-Girlfriend whom you have given up on because it was too much...

* Stay together for the future of your couple life.

* A knight that must save the Princess...

* You and she are doing it together... Despite the challenges of...

* Children playing together to be adult...

* A passenger, without a ticket and controller, who wishes to locate her

She will want to do the Role Play. By setting the goal, the Role Play will dictate your future actions.

The Perfect Date will let you focus on what to say, and what topics, so there's no need to worry about that.

Roleplay makes it easier to pull and push or use other seduction methods. It is possible to have physical contact or an obedience test, and everything will be much easier.

For example, if you ask them to visualize a Role-Play with you getting married, you could take her hand and make a gesture of slipping it (physical contact + Pull) and then say "this is too tight...mmh...are you fat?" (Push) Then, while you are giving your hand to her, tell her that it is up to you to take hers (test of obedience + personal contact). To do these things in a Role Play setting would be too difficult. The Role Play makes it easy because it is a game. The result will be identical, as you have increased the attraction using the Pull and Push and Physical Contact.

Role-Playing refers to a game. This fantasy game allows you to do whatever you want. Although it may seem odd at first glance it is actually quite fun and will be loved by your child.

The date doesn't have be solely based on the roleplaying game. You could create additional role-playing gaming games and bring one into the play when it is available. Or, one sentence might be sufficient. Make sure to include at least one of these elements. Because it is important to have a purpose in your date.

These are the main objectives of Role-Playing Games.

* Add malice. If you are in a scene that involves sex, it is likely she will imagine it. This image will work in your favor until it becomes reality.

* He behaves naturally without any worries or blockages, such as the judgement of others or the fear of doing something wrong. You will see her as a person who is comfortable with this behavior and she will allow you to meet her.

Role Game logic and rationality are completely out of place. She can play along and fight back or interrupt the Role

Play. You cannot answer logically while you are still in the game.

Example.

You will ask her (while she takes her hand): "Will it be a dance, Princess?" Will it not be an incognito lady cleaning? I don't have enough time to clean up his mess with shoes and mice. The time constraints are also a problem.

She: "How dare YOU! I am a real princess. I can do all I want.

You: "It'sn't like that, I was just joking, ..." OVER!

Role Play should not be used to justify anything you do.

Don't be so stupid, use logic. Your Role Play experience has been destabilizing. After you created a scene with physical contact, and then you discredited and retracted what you had constructed. The rational part of your brain should be disabled. If you get too emotional, it is best to forget about it. You don't have to destroy the work you've done. Just get to the point.

You could have responded like that:

You will take her, hug and dance 2 steps. Let's check if the Princess can dance... which frog is capable of doing this? Then, you can disconnect yourself (push). Just in case ..." it wouldn't be so.

Or you can interrupt it all by saying:

You:

If you'd like, you can re-engage in the Role Play if needed. So, while you may have passed the Shit Test (destabilizing phrase), you have not destroyed your Role Play.

When you jokes are too pushy, she becomes embarrassed or seems offended. So you just say "joking". If you are able to touch her stomach, kiss her cheeks or grab her hand, let her know that you didn't mean it. You were doing well until you heard "sorry/joke" which was enough to bring out your slavish side. The created sexual tension can be destroyed with just one word. t's important. Please read it again. You don't have to be embarrassed of your instincts or desires.

Another example. A showcase for a travel agency.

You say: "Imagine me on a deserted sandy beach like that... there is no one looking at and you can do anything you want... Can swimming be possible?" (Free of judgments)

She: "It'd be great... ofcourse I can swim!"

You: "Excellent. Then I take with me one condition... (you determine)

She: "Let's listen... What is it?"

You: "You should bring sunscreen... so that I can spread it onto my back...touch... listen?" I have delicate skin."

She: "Ah-ah deal, i put on the superbronzer"

You: "full tan! We are just you and me. We sunbathe, swim and swim naked.

She: "What? But I am ashamed." She imagines that you are naked together.

You say, "then I'll go leave you at home!"

Another example. Sex and Relationship Department in the sex shop bookcase.

You:

She: "What?"

You: "In truth, our lesbian relationship is over. You want me to work less and get bored. I'll let you go... ("From something hypothetical, you go to the current and you decide).

She "ah,ah no cute, I give you up. You prefer to spend all day with your boobs than giving me attention."

You: "Didn't you feel my boobs?" They are stunning! ... and not only those!" (spin about)

You (hold her hand): "I understand. "All we need is couple therapy." (Physical Contact)

Move to the Psychology Department. You can keep playing, start another game, or talk to someone about what you really want. She will have imagined herself having a relationship and sleeping with you. As I already mentioned, you can only imagine your environment (library and shopping centre) as if it were your own. Can be used in the same way as if they were found in many places.

Now it's your turn. Play with your imagination and don't use logic to stop the sexual tension!

Role-playing simulates a scenario that does not exist in real life. This includes no interstellar travel, flying elephants, or aliens. The date is not a set of sexual conjectures. This date is intended to allow you to get to understand each other.

In the end, don't say foolish or weird things in the Role Play. Instead, think about how you can enjoy time with her.

Chapter 5: Dating To Your Own Terms

If you've completed the previous five chapters, volume dating will benefit you. You will be receiving a constant supply date. You would think that this is a good thing. But, it opens up the can of worms.

It is too easy to fall for bad habits. Maybe you are in recovery from a bad past relationship. Perhaps you are in a new relationship. Perhaps you have never been in a serious relationship. No matter your situation, be open to dating on your terms. Don't feel like you must make certain decisions just because others expect you to. Do not feel you must feel a certain way just because you feel it is necessary.

It is important to remember that, at the very least in the beginning stages, dating is about you. If you aren't comfortable, or if you're having fun, it's time to end the relationship.

Here are a few tips for repeat dates once you've been on a date with someone.

To begin with, you must avoid codependency. It's easy to become so engrossed in the excitement of a relationship that you feel you can't do without it. You're welcome to enjoy the romance of being in love. But, keep your head. Never ever lose your head. Codependency is possible if you don't let your guard down.

A codependent lifestyle is bad news. There is no such thing a person you can't live without. That is bunk. You only feel this way because you have allowed yourself to feel it. No such person exists in real life. If you feel an initial rush of emotion, it is important to be honest about what you're feeling.

Also, you should be aware that you could be being used. There are many men who use dating sites to search for women. We're not talking just about finances and sexuality; we're also referring to emotional matters.

Many men are emotional consumers. They may be very narcissistic/depressed, and nothing makes them happier than to share their misery with others. Others men are emotional sadistic. They are dealing trauma from the past. The trick to their success is to narrate this trauma in a false narrative that requires them to include participants. It's very abusive and bizarre. Even if there's nothing physical happening, this is one of the most abusive relationships you will ever find.

The truth is that people can inflict injury on your body. But your body will soon heal. When your heart hurts and your mind is damaged it takes longer to heal. It is sometimes impossible to get the genie back in the bottle after it has been taken.

How to determine if you are using him

I wish I could tell my readers that this game is only one-sided. Although I wish that I could tell it was only the bad guys abusing women and using them, it is actually the reverse. Be honest with yourself. It is abuse to just enjoy the company of these guys. This is also a form or using.

Keep in mind that they also have expectations. You may have heard me say that the entire process is about you at the beginning. But this does not allow you to abuse people. Respect each others' autonomy and needs.

You have to keep this person around because they are obviously doing something for your at some point. It's okay to show enough respect to that person that you don't want them to use your name. Make it mutually enriching, and uplifting.

Remember, having fun is the key to success.

The whole point behind dating is having fun. It should be reciprocal. It must be mutually beneficial and comforting. But there comes a time when the fun is over and you must decide what your next steps are. That is when you decide to take it to another level. Mutuality is vital. Both you and your partner must desire to reach the next level. It's not one-sided.

Be aware that your relationships will become all about you if you stop looking at them as just you.

Second, it's fine to want something other than what you have. It's okay for you to want to move along, but be open to the possibility of resentful feelings. Do not think that you want to be a slave to this person. This is anti-social, and it's pathological behavior.

Safe dating tips

Let me explain if this isn't obvious. It is vital to have safe and secure relationships with men. Physical safety is what you should be doing.

Your emotional safety and security are equally important. Keep in mind what you're getting into. To ensure that nobody is hurt, make sure you clearly define your expectations. While it might feel good for women to get back at men after being hurt in the past by a man, consider yourself the other half of the equation. It's not good to be at one end of such games.

Do yourself a favor by being emotionally safe. Be realistic about what you are doing, and stick to safe limits. Respect the other person if you want to be loved. To feel loved, appreciated and valued, you have to first love and accept yourself. Then you can show this to others.

Chapter 6: Conversing With Women And Getting Dates

Fear of appearing creepy is a negative side effect of dating. This keeps many men from feeling confident and like themselves around women they are attracted. Most men are aware of the fact that women tend not to choose the right men for them. This only makes it more difficult for men to stand out among the rest. I don't mean to sound desperate or pathetic. It's quite a burden on poor men trying for a date, especially if they are looking for a woman who is attractive. These men are unable to try and avoid women due to all of the pressure. Instead of enduring a painful rejection, they simply accept that they don't have the potential to date. Please do not do this. It is time to find a middle ground. How?

Introvert men can find it overwhelming to be involved in such an environment. If you are one these people, you can probably see in detail the worst-case scenarios that could occur after you approach a girl. Instead of getting lost in all the details and thinking that you are making mistakes by moving forward, it is better to ignore the negativity and just approach the woman! You can easily become lost in the misery of others and live in unnecessary fear. It may be hard to break free from the negative thoughts but it is possible. These fears that you hold on to are often the result of an overactive imagination. They are not real. This section will explain how you can approach and speak to women.

Undesirable Behavior

Avoid certain behavior if you don't want to be seen as creepy. This includes situations in which your words, actions or words make her feel uneasy or even threatened.

It's exactly what you don't want her to feel. She feels like you are pushing her boundaries. These are the things you must avoid saying or doing at all cost.

* Engaging in sex conversations with unrequited partners.

* Sharing inappropriate images with her.

* Absolute disregard for her physical borders.

These are just three ways that you can make a woman feel uncomfortable. Women have to deal with this type of man many times in their lifetime. You can say goodbye to any chance you had of having a good relationship with her.

When to Approach

This is a problem that many men struggle with. To avoid coming across as creepy or nonthreatening, men tend to avoid women. This can be frightening for women. You can meet and talk to anyone if you do not find it strange. It is the only way humans interact and get along with each other. There are certain times and places you can and cannot approach women. Allow your intuition and judgments to guide you in such situations. Here are some things you should keep in your mind.

Locate

If you do not intend to appear creepy, even accidentally, the first thing you need is to consider the setting. You might approach a woman in a sunny park, but not in a darkly lit alleyway while she is walking home at evening. In some cases, like bars and clubs, people are expecting to be approached with the opposite kind of sex. Women are more likely to be afraid of strangers approaching them in the dark than men. It's important to be aware of the context and the venue. At a funeral, flirting with someone is frowned upon. But, at a wedding, this is possible.

Never Leave Her Behind

When approaching a woman, keep these points in your mind. But don't make her feel trapped. Always be mindful of how you approach her. It's normal to speak to a woman at the beach. If you approach the same woman at the motel's laundromat or motel, however, it might seem threatening. Even if it isn't your intention to confront her, you can make it seem dangerous by blocking her entrance or closing the door. These are all simple rules to keep in mind when approaching a woman. Just be aware of your surroundings and the circumstances.

Respect Her Privacy

It is okay to not approach a woman if you feel uncomfortable. You should not intrude on her space unless she consents.

As stated earlier, make it a habit to allow her to have free access and space to go where she pleases.

Conversational Strategies

We are constantly told that Mars is the home of men and Venus the home for women. Many people think that women and men have very little in common. Here are some tips that will help you have a pleasant and productive conversation with women.

Looking Beyond the Facade

We are all skin and bones with individual personalities underneath. Everyone has baggage, and each of us can be haunted by our past. You don't have to be all that things. People don't like to be reminded of the unpleasant things about their past, or any difficult events. You must be able see through the woman's facade when you speak to her. You need to take the time to get her to open up and understand her. Whatever your background, it is important to have a real connection with her before you try to chat.

Building Common Ground

To build understanding, you should take the time to identify common points. This skill can be useful in all areas of your life that you need to interact. You could, for example, go to a grocery store or other places where you can interact with others. You can find out something about the checkout staff when you reach the counter. Personal experience has shown that women often spend a lot more time and effort dressing up. When you see that someone you have met has some nice accessories, don't be afraid to compliment her. This will immediately make the other person stop doing whatever and give you a compliment.

Let Her Talk

It is very easy to do. You don't need to appear brilliant or incredible. Just be a good listener, and let her speak. Be attentive and not distracted while listening to her. Keep your responses to the subject in mind. It is that easy. You might have complimented a woman's accessory in the example above, which opened the door for conversation. You can start a conversation by sharing some information about the accessory with her, like "I bought this for my birthday!". You don't want to start talking about yourself. Be clear that you are trying get her to speak to you. It's easy to learn this trick after a few attempts.

Avoid Certain Topics

You should avoid any subject that can lead to disagreement. To make someone dislike you, the simplest way to do it is to take a contrary view and tell them they're wrong. Let's suppose that the woman we used as an example agreed to have coffee with you. This is an important step. So, congratulations! You don't have to impress her by being smart or strong. This could mean that the last cup of coffee you share together will be the last. Instead, you should find topics you both enjoy discussing.

I would suggest you to avoid politics if you don't agree on it. Until you feel comfortable with each other, you can continue to disagree about any topic. You should avoid any topics that spark passions or strong opinions. Avoid sexy and unwholesome topics. Avoid all topics that may cause a heated argument. Remember that both you and she have the right of opinion. But, the goal is to communicate with her. A disagreement will destroy any chance that you might have.

Never invade her private space

Respect her space. Don't get too close and don't try blocking her body. Keep an arm's reach between the two of them. While you can lean toward her for conversation, it is best to keep your distance.

Personal Hygiene Is Important

Before you approach a woman, brush your teeth. Bad breath can make a conversation end much quicker than other things. You can stop the conversation by having a cup or two of coffee before you begin to talk. You should always have some mints with your wherever you go. You must take care of your hygiene. Your appearance is all about how you present your self.

Get her number

Try to identify common points with her once you have started talking. You may share a mutual love for an artist, like the same cuisine, or have a common hobby. Don't lose this little bit of information. This can be brought up casually later on in the conversation. For example, if she mentions that she likes Mexican food, you can say something like "I know this little Mexican restaurant that you would love." This is an easy way to request her number. It is also non-threatening.

Once you have the number you need, you can start messaging her. Start a conversation with her by dropping a brief message. You will see how she responds. If she responds quickly and tries continuing the conversation, that's your green signal. Be sure to not send her unsuitable messages and don't text too often.

Let me end with a final tip: If she does not feel interested in you then it is time to move on. If she signals to your in any way that she isn't interested in continuing the conversation then it is time to say farewell. Even though you may be a lovely person, if she isn't interested in you continuing the conversation, you need to find another person. You shouldn't let one rejection devastate your self-confidence.

You can have easy conversations and smooth interactions with women if you keep these simple tips in view. But you'll need to practice this a few more times until you get the hang.

Chapter 7: If The Girl Would Like You

If you use the strategies and steps in this book, your natural behavior will be the same as it was before. You will be more confident. You will be content to know that you don't have need to persuade or deceive a woman into liking you.

You've been on a first date. Perhaps you've been on a couple of dates. You have built a solid connection based on honesty and communication. You like her and she loves you.

Now, what if the woman asks you to marry her?

What if she is looking to elevate things? How will you be able to tell?

How to determine if a woman would like to go further

There are signs that indicate whether a woman wants to go farther. While it's the best signal, it can be hard for women to tell you. Many women won't be as bold to ask you to kiss her. Very few will even say they want to sex with your man.

Here's how you can tell when a lady might be ready to move on:

Body language

The first sign that a woman wants to pursue something further is her body language.

If she leans in toward you all the time, it is a sign that she is truly interested. She wants to interact more with you. Other signs could indicate she is begging you to kiss her. When they want you to kiss them, women tend to bring their lips closer to yours.

Contacts with the eyes

If she is truly interested in you, a woman may make constant eye contact with you if she is. If she's making eye contact with me, that is a good sign.

Other than her eyes meeting with yours, another signal is her eyes meeting with your lips. If a woman wants to kiss you, she will not only direct eye contact with her but will also look down at your lips occasionally.

Laughing and smiling a lot

A woman who smiles at you means she's enjoying being with you. You can tell if she smiles, laughs, and keeps her eyes open when she's smiling. Even though she might not be wanting to get in bed, it is a sign that things are moving in the right direction.

Physical contact

It doesn't matter if she knows it or not, physical contact will tell you that she is very comfortable around you. You might also notice other signals that she is interested in moving on to the next stage. She may feel comfortable enough to allow you to kiss her. She may feel comfortable enough to have some sex with your partner. This isn't a signal to her to be aggressive. This might mean that she's open and willing to talk about it or do it if necessary.

We have some suggestions for you

If a woman shows multiple signals to you but you're not sure if it was clear, then one thing you can do is to listen to her verbal cues about what she wants.

She might talk about a close friend that had a sex encounter and hint at her thoughts. She might tell you, "I generally don't feel sexual feelings about anybody quickly."

This isn't an indication to be rude or push her. This is an opportunity for you to answer by continuing the conversation. Ask her what you want from a sexual encounter. If she's asking for you, it will be a conversation that leads to the question "Do you wish to have sex?"

It shouldn't make her feel weird or embarrassed by the question. This question serves two purposes. This question lets women know what you want. It lets a woman know what you want. Even though she may not be ready to have sex, tomorrow might be different. Second, it shows respect. Your asking will make her feel more respected than you kissing and taking off her clothes.

You can follow the conversation to what you want if she gives direct hints. If she gives you signals that were valid, continue the conversation.

Asking you questions about it

When she asks questions, this is another sign that a woman is giving verbal clues. If she begins to question you about your intentions and you don't have the "move", this is the perfect chance to ask her questions and give her your answer. She may directly ask you if it's something that you might consider having sex.

These questions should be asked honestly. Don't run away. Don't be timid. If she asks you whether you've ever considered having sex, and you say yes, then gauge your response. If she responds positively to your question, smiles, giggles or is smiling, then you will know exactly what she wants. Ask her the exact same question if she doesn't answer. If she answers positively, ask her if you can continue. However, it will depend on where you live and how prepared. If you're going somewhere, this is a good time to ask her whereabouts. You might be at your place now.

You can gauge her interest

All these signals, conversations, or questions are designed to gauge interest in her desires. But, it is important to be completely honest with her about the things you want.

You might be dating someone who is very shy. If this is true, you might try asking her some soft questions regarding intimacy and sexual relationships. Talk to your woman about what you think about intimacy and romance. The woman will feel more comfortable speaking up about this topic with you. It's unlikely that a woman will feel embarrassed if you have been sincere with her and treated her with respect. She may not have felt the same way if you weren't honest with her. Lucky for you, she is comfortable with you being confident.

The best way to maintain open and honest communication between you two is to gauge your woman's interest.

Chapter 8: Know When To Make Your Move

No matter how wealthy, attractive or rich you might be, it's your responsibility to approach a female. Expect a woman not to approach you.

Many men feel single because it is not their job to be proactive. Some men only focus on their work, education, and business. Many men complain that they cannot find the woman of their dreams. What chance do you have of finding the woman you desire?

Women, even those who are extremely interested in your career, will rarely make the first move. If you hesitate when she shows interest in you, it will indicate that you lack confidence. And, as we mentioned before, women are very sensitive to a lack of confidence.

Every man should have the confidence and ability to approach any woman, start a conversation, and be confident in his abilities. Approach anxiety is something many men struggle with. This causes them to never move. How many times did you see a woman that you wanted pass you, but she froze?

It is important to have courage and not be afraid of approaching women. It is important to overcome fear of rejection. Even if she rejects you, you must feel proud that you took the initiative. To overcome anxiety, you must do it. It's easier to do it the more you do.

I suffered from anxiety and approach disorder. My past experiences have made me a stronger person. In the past, when I met a woman who I liked, my anxiety and nervousness would make me nervous. Because many women could sense and feel the anxiousness and nervousness in my energy, body language, and energy, they rejected and dismissed me.

These experiences made me more determined than ever to master this aspect of my life. Despite my fear, though, I was determined to be the man making a move. I wanted to meet as many women as possible until I became better at it. I was afraid of meeting women I liked but couldn't make a move due to fearful thoughts and analysis paralysis. I would return home feeling completely defeated after such encounters. I felt extremely bad about myself, and it wasn't just that. I felt depressed and felt that there was something wrong.

When I saw friends who were extremely confident with women being rejected, my mentality changed. My friends taught me that they did not let the rejection affect their self-worth and that they moved on quickly. They were happy even when they were rejected. They did not let their rejection define who and what they were. The next day they were out talking to new women. Each time I was turned down, I never wanted to be rejected again. I would suffer for months in emotional pain before I was able to move on.

As I set out on self-growth I realized that I was worthy and that being rejected by a woman didn't make me weak. This realization was made more real when I realized that rejections are a part of life. Celebrities get rejected all the while Jesus Christ was rejected by many. This helped me realize that I was not an exception and that not every woman that I met would choose to be with my. I'm sure some would reject my proposal, but that is okay because rejection is part in life.

Every woman you meet may not agree with you. Rejoice in the fact that she was approached. Feel happy that you approached the woman. I can smile and be happy when a woman rejects my approach. At least there's no regret. It's better than failing to try, rather than not trying at all. Do not allow women you like to walk past your house. Do your best to be proactive. If you fail, you'll know that you tried.

Understanding the importance of having the highest fear of failure will help you grow. Fear will always lead you. The thing that you are most afraid is the one you need to learn. If you have a full time job and are always busy, make a commitment to meet at least two women each weekend. When you do, you'll find a woman that likes you just like you like her. Being able to meet many women opens doors and allows you to have a variety of options. If you have many women to choose form your circle of friends, you won't feel as needy as if you were pursuing one girl.

9.1: How to Meet Women

Because you know the type of woman that you desire (the list you created previously), and because you must meet women in order to be proactive about approaching them, here are some places where you can meet and ask women out.

* Seminars

* Conferences

* Grocery Stores

* Nightclubs

* Wedding/Marriage ceremonies

* Bars

* Shopping Malls

* On the Street

* Church

* At work

* Sports events

* The gym

* Club

* In School

* University campuses

* Restaurants

* Public/Private swimming pools

* Lounges

* Farmers markets

* Yoga class

* Concerts

* Coffee shops

* Bookstores

* Comedy clubs

* Niche events for business

* Niche hobby events

* Beaches

* Art shows

* Private Parties

* Trade shows

* Social events

Always remember to have fun. Take your family to places they love and do what you love. Your ideal woman will have interests that are similar to yours. It's easier for women with similar interests to engage in meaningful conversations. These are just a few of the many reasons you can meet women almost anywhere. Start taking action now. Go out and meet as much women as you can.

9.2 How to Approach Women

Your first encounter with a woman is critical. If you don't do it correctly, it will impact your chances of securing a relationship with her. It will be much easier to date a woman if you have a good first experience with her.

You will need to work hard to change the woman's opinion you have formed about her. If, for example, you are perceived as lacking confidence by a woman in your first interaction it may be difficult to get her open up. Sometimes it is better just to move on, even if you were not happy at the beginning of your interaction. This lesson was hard for me.

I met many women during my self-growth dating/relationship journey. Although the first interaction wasn't good, because I was so attracted, I kept trying. Since the more I tried, the more women rejected me, the more I was tested.

Women who had a good start are the ones I have had success with. It's important that you make a good first impression. It's better not to start badly and then make mistakes later. If she gets a positive impression of you, she will often forgive later mistakes. However, if you have weaknesses in the beginning, it may be difficult for her to give your chance unless you are highly attracted.

You can tolerate mistakes if a woman is attracted more to you than you are. However, if the attraction between you and her is low or average, there's no way you can win. Don't waste your time. Instead, walk away so you can give another woman the chance. Although it is not impossible to have a great interaction from the beginning, I do not believe that it will be easy to turn that into something extraordinary. Although it does happen, these cases are uncommon and usually require a lot from the man.

I said previously that you should never allow a woman you like to pass by you. I suggested that you boldly ask her out and make your move. Here are some steps that will help you do this.

#1: Take control of your approach

Approach her from the front, rather than the back. It's not your goal to scare her. Your goal should be to lower her guard.

#2: Smile

Smile at her and try to make her feel comfortable.

#3: Eye contact

Maintain good eye contact.

#4: Confidence

Be confident

#5 - Be aware of how you approach things

You should ask for her name using strong vocal tones. Then wait for her to respond. Do not ask her for your name. Instead, just say, "Well Stephanie. It's nice to have you." You are trying to communicate her attraction.

A woman who inquires to know your name is likely to be more attracted towards you than one who doesn't. Never underestimate a woman's attraction level. The goal of your first encounter with a woman you love is to judge her level and attraction. If you think she is attracted to you, get her phone number and contact information.

#6: Keep a mystery air

Be mysterious and let her tell the story. It is a common mistake that men make when they first meet a woman: they reveal too much about themselves and are counterproductive to their attraction. Don't volunteer information; let her dig it out of you.

Women like mystery. You can't be trusted to tell the truth about yourself. It will make it difficult for women to accept a date. In the past, I have made similar mistakes. These women did not offer me the chance of a date. They knew everything about me since our first meeting. There was little excitement.

I was once surprised by the amount of information men give her about themselves, according to a woman. She shared with me how she took men's interest too seriously when they showed her too much interest.

Today, my dating motto says it all: "If she didn't ask me, I won't tell." I only give information to women if she requests it. If she doesn't want to ask, then I withhold the information. This has proved to be extremely successful. If I am more mysterious, women are more likely to want to learn more about me. My success rate in attracting women to me is higher when I am more mysterious than when I reveal everything about myself.

It doesn't matter what you prove to a woman. A woman does not care about your outstanding record, acts, kindness, or good deeds. She wants to know more about herself. It is difficult for women to trust men who constantly tell them about their accomplishments.

I met a woman once who instantly felt attracted to me. I told her so much about me and my accomplishments during our first interaction. I thought it would make her more attractive. As you can see, my revelations had no effect on her attraction towards me. She distrusted me and doubted me even more.

Let me remind you that when you meet a woman who you like, she should do most of her talking. It's really not about you. It's about her. Talking too much about herself is a sure-fire way to get her to stop liking you. If she is not interested in learning more about you, don't divulge any personal information. This one simple change can lead to great success in your dating relationships.

A second benefit of not divulging personal information to a woman is the ability to see how much attraction you have for her. If a woman does not ask questions about you, that means she has low attraction for you. For such women to be interested in you, you'll need to work very hard for a date. The goal is to meet women who are interested and have expressed an interest in you. It's much more enjoyable to date a woman that is interested in you, than to date one who is not.

#7: Have fun and play!

Talk to her, or joke with them. You should be playful. You will have high success rates if you are able to make her laugh during the first date. Women like humor. Women love to laugh and will feel more positive about you if you can make them smile.

#8: Make a date now

Set up a date when you are certain of your attraction to her. I'll ask you questions such as "How is your schedule today?" or "What about tomorrow?" depending on the time that we met. Usually, I ask women whether they are free.

Once she says she is free, you could then say, "Let's have a drink at XXXX place at seven o'clock in the evening." Once she has agreed to meet at the time and place, you can give her your number. Then, get hers. This is a good strategy since once she has accepted to go on an intimate date with you it's easy to give her her phone number.

NOTE: If your confidence is low, get her number so you can call to set up a date. It is not for getting to know her, but setting dates.

Calling her or texting her should have the sole purpose of setting dates. Romantic attraction comes from real interactions with a woman, not just chit-chatting on the phone. It's possible to touch, hug, hold hands, kiss and even make eye contact when you meet a woman in person. It's difficult to seduce someone via a communication device. It is important to plan physical dates together so your attraction grows.

If she does not answer the phone, it is usually a sign of her disinterest in you. It is rare for a woman to say bluntly, "I cannot give your number because I don't like you that way." Most women use indirect means to refuse. Some women will give your number if they insist.

One time I asked a woman to give me her phone number. Her reply was "I will give that to you when I meet again." So I asked her "How sure are your chances of meeting again?" I have it now so it's easier to reach you," she said. After I called her, all of my calls went through to voice mail. She didn't pick up. I tried to send her text messages but she didn't reply. She gave me her number as a way to get rid.

Most men make the fatal mistake of insisting on meeting a woman with such behavior, and then chasing after her. I have made this mistake.

It doesn't make a woman interested in your pursuit of her if she isn't interested in it. You will only drive her away if you pursue her after she shows her disinterest. A woman who is willing to give you her mobile number without hesitation is a great prospect. Only meet women who are open to dating you.

#9 - For dates that can be set by phone

If she did give you her number, but it wasn't immediately set a date, wait three working days before calling her. Men tend to call women immediately after receiving her number. Some men even begin calling her multiple times per day. This destroys anticipation and diminishes mystery.

Let's say that you met her on Saturday. She gave you her number. To schedule a Saturday meeting, call her Wednesday or Thursday of next week. A definite date is when you have a set time, day and place.

Don't let things go. Do not say, "Let's have a Saturday meeting" or "Let's have a Saturday at Thomas Bar." Instead say, "Let's have a Saturday at Thomas Bar at 7PM." This is more precise and is easier for her to accept. Women like direct men. It is possible that the woman will call you first and you can then set up a date. The ideal situation is one where a woman reaches out to you first. This will allow you to put your focus on setting dates.

Chapter 9: Tips For Confidence

Your Walk is your Masterpiece

Women are more interested in what you wear than your walking style. Don't forget to dress nicely and to pay attention how you stand and walk. Do you rush everywhere you go? You should slow down. A confident person isn't in hurry. Confident people have a clear understanding of what they are talking about and where they are walking. Walk as if you know exactly where your destination is and why.

Confidence

Take compliments from women on your eyes and smile with confidence. Confident people will accept compliments. But insecure people will not. Insecure people may respond with doubts or list reasons why the compliment wasn't true. This can be offensive and make the friend uncomfortable.

When to call

If a woman gives her her phone number, you must call her within two business days or you will look foolish or scared. To make yourself feel more confident, pretend that you're calling a business. You can think of your date as trying for a job. This can take the pressure off of your current job.

Voicemail

People aren't likely to leave voice messages these day, so be bold and stand out. If you want to appear confident, your voice should be moderately loud. If you stand, you could hum and make the call. You will be able to raise your voice to a natural and appealing pitch. Make sure you tell her who you are, what you were doing, and why. Instead of asking if she'd be interested in getting together, ask her when is most convenient.

Don't be discouraged

Negative comments about yourself are not something you should be doing. Instead, think about your positive qualities and hobbies and make it a happy topic. It's important to talk about the positive things that you are proud and eager to share with others. You should be wary of someone who starts talking down about themselves when you first meet them.

Be mindful

Try to keep your back to a woman when you're sitting down to talk to her. Try to be at her side, rather than sitting directly in front. This allows her to move in a way that will allow you to see her side. Many women don't feel comfortable being confronted in frontal assault by sitting opposite someone. This lets you gauge her interest. If she turns her face to you, it is a sign that she wants to spend time with you.

Chapter 10: The Vulcans Were On To Something

Any productive conversation or argument must be able flow without getting sidetracked.

Imagine a brainstorming session at work. All ideas should be accepted. Nothing should be rejected. If this train is stopped, negativity will ensue, creative juices stop flowing, and judgment will take root.

Let's start this chapter again for you and your woman.

What stops your creative nature from flowing when you have any kind of dispute with your lady? Leading with "no". Telling her she is lying, or telling her she's wrong. Telling her she's crazy. I would bet every burrito she makes that she has done it to me. What was your reaction to that? Probably anger and frustration.

You will do more than hinder your own productive nature if you do these things. You will most likely cause your woman to feel upset or even to start a conflict by responding negatively. It adds an adversarial tone to any conversation.

It's one such slippery slope where you don't even know you're on the path to a jarring absence of communication until it becomes obvious that you haven't had the opportunity to productively address a particular issue in 6 months.

You can avoid going too far down that slippery slope by not saying "no". Instead, be clear and direct. This would take you a lot.

Put in a "no-interruptions" rule so she can speak her whole piece and you can listen without having to defend yourself.

The Vulcans were on to something.

You may have now noticed one of my communication themes.

It's to remove emotion from decisions and arguments, since they aren't helpful to the goal. Women often respond with anger or shut down. Star Trek lore reveals that the rational, emotionless Vulcans likely had some great, productive disagreements.

That's precisely what this chapter focuses on. Emotional outbursts and decisions that are emotional don't result in good things. Just like the saying "Nothing is good after 2AM "..." and "Only great things happen after 3AM ,"...," "Nothing is good in emotional arguments."

Emotions are often the diametric opposing of logic. Emotions limit logic, cause tangential and personal attacks, and can lead to a fogged mind that has little understanding of its consequences. Extreme reactions and declarations are common, but most often nothing gets done.

The best way to deal with a situation is to usually walk away, calm down, then allow yourself to feel more in control and balanced. It is possible to even go to sleep about it.

It is easy to recognize that this is the right option when we feel emotionally unstable. But how about actually realizing that you're there?

This is the main battle, but it's also the hardest.

If you find yourself angry, you can take a step back, breathe deeply, and reflect on what caused it. It's possible to see your situation objectively and have your emotions calm down.

We prefer solving problems than just listening.

You will know at this point who you want for specific situations.

Talking to your father is a good option if you are looking for someone to talk to about your emotional issues. Perhaps your only friend who is an accountant can help you with money problems. You may have one college buddy who played flag football with, and they know how terrible your football team is doing.

Or maybe you have a really bad rant you want to let out. Perhaps your friend is all about action and taking steps.

It's important for you to recognize that this will not be your woman's instinct.

It's one of those gendered stereotypes that is true for me time after time... and sometimes I have to fight it myself.

If a man hears about a problem, it is likely that his natural instinct will be to fix it. If a woman hears about a problem, it is more likely that she will offer emotional validation and empathy.

This may speak to one of two fundamental differences between men, women and men: the functional or emotional focus. Whatever the reason, it should be used to temper expectations from the women in your life.

The majority of women who rant want to be heard and validated. It's not all about solving the problem, or even taking action. This is not our natural tendency. We listen, and we care about their views... but it might not make sense to talk about the problem as if it solves the underlying problem.

You should not let your woman vent to you. She may simply want to talk and vent rather than brainstorming solutions.

Emotional intimacy requires more work than bench pressing 300 lbs.

It's not surprising that women are more emotionally intuitive and in tune than men.

This fact is undisputed. Therefore, we cannot expect men to have the same emotional openness and intuition as women. The title of this chapter says that emotional intimacy is harder than bench pressing 300 lbs because of how we were conditioned by society.

This means that your manhood in western society expects you to be strong, stoic and unbending.

Don't be afraid not to ask her more open-ended questions. Instead, take the time to reflect on what makes you tick. Ask yourself why your do certain things and what your views are on certain issues. Think back to your childhood. Consider taking a genuine interest in your motivations and how they drive you each day. And then, tell her.

It is likely to make you uncomfortable.

There are very few people that have ever done something like that with you. Perhaps you stumble upon something that is a catharsis to yourself. It might be something you haven't shared with anyone before. She will feel compelled and motivated to share the emotional glasnost and you'll instantly become more intimate and connected.

Just because society has made us feel obligated to suppress our emotional needs does not mean we aren't capable of having them and enjoy sharing them.

The beauty of sharing your vulnerability with someone is to be vulnerable together.

Chapter 11: Online Dating Confidence: How To Boost And Maintain It

We've always noted in this book that being authentic with your partner is key to online dating success.

A man must possess a high level of self-belief to be authentic. It is important to believe in yourself and have faith in your abilities.

Being authentic and true to your self is essential. You also need to believe in the love you deserve, know your worth and believe you have the potential to be loved.

Why confidence is important

Chante Salick (a relationship and dating coach) says confidence is a crucial ingredient whose availability or lack will determine your online dating success.

She then points out that online dating is difficult because of a lack in confidence. Instead of looking at the challenge positively, you start to see it through a negative lens -- a monologue about "all the reasons why online dating is so bad" -- which can make negative online dating experiences more likely.

Coach Chante says that this narrative plays out in your mind when you approach any kind of dating, even online dating. It changes the energy that permeates online and offline interactions and makes them feel negative. You are more likely to express insecurity, neediness, or other negative feelings to the women you choose to date with a long-term relationship.

Conversely, being confident and certain will make you more attractive, sensual as well as balanced.

You will likely be all these things and it will reflect in how you approach women online, as well how you handle your interactions. Furthermore, your verbal and/or nonverbal communication will be influenced by the positive energy from feeling worthy, balanced, and capable.

After talking about how important it is to be confident when you are online dating and how this can help increase your chances for finding love, let's now discuss how to cultivate confidence.

3 Easy Ways to Improve Your Dating Confidence

This will help you increase your confidence in dating

#: Cultivate self-awareness

This nerve-wracking experience can lead to fearful emotions, such as trying to match strangers and starting conversations.

If you don't take the time to be aware of yourself and your negative emotions, you will likely feel the same as an untrained archer blindfolded.

To be more self-aware, you need to learn how to recognize your inner critic and calm it down before it becomes a ferocious, insurmountable beast. Knowing yourself, your fears, preconceptions and negative beliefs will help you recognize when you are hindering your chances of finding love and/or being with a great lady.

#: Prioritize yourself

Making compromises is an essential part of building successful relationships. You may feel like you're competing with a million other men for the attention and love you desire. It is easy, however, to compromise the things that make your uniqueness and bring you joy.

When you go online dating, confidence is about feeling confident. You can instill this feeling of wellbeing by prioritizing the things you love.

Negative conversations with women, "ghosting", and rejection should not define who you are as an individual. Be positive and keep your cool. Don't let rejection, negative conversations with women, "ghosting," or bad dates define who you are as a person. Take a pledge that for every five online matches you sign up for, you will treat you to a solo date in which you do something you enjoy.

#: Swipe, match, message, meet, repeat

Are you ready for the truth bomb? Here it comes:

We can simplify online dating down to five steps: Swipe first, match second, message then meet up again. This is all there is!

Keep this simple five-step process in your head and you will be able to use it again and again until you find the right partner. Do not let a few failed attempts turn into a huge deal. Instead, "swipe" and then message, message, match, meet, repeat.

You can stay focused and grounded as you navigate the online dating world. Do not idolize women.

It will help you boost your confidence by being aware of the potential dating scams that you could encounter during this process.

Chapter 12: How To Get Dates And Converse With Women

Fear of appearing creepy is a negative side effect of dating. Many men are unable to feel confident and at ease around women they find attractive. Most men are aware of the fact that women tend not to choose the right men for them. This creates more pressure for men to stand out among the rest. I mean it in a positive way, not in a way that is pathetic or depressed. It's quite a burden on poor men who try to find a date for a girl they are only interested in. These men are unable to try and avoid women due to all of the pressure. Instead of enduring a painful rejection, they simply accept that they don't have the potential to date. Please do not do this. It is time to find a middle ground. How?

Introvert men can find it overwhelming to be involved in such an environment. If you're one these guys, then you know all about the worst-case scenarios that could occur when you approach a girl. Instead of getting lost in all the details and thinking that you are making mistakes by moving forward, it is better to ignore the negative and just approach the woman! You can easily become lost in the misery of others and live in fear. It may be hard to let go of this negative thought process. Many fears that you hold on to are the result of an overactive imagination. They are not real. You'll learn how to approach and speak with women in this section.

Undesirable Behavior

Avoid certain behavior if you don't want to be seen as a creep. This includes situations where your words, actions or words make her feel uneasy or threatened. It's exactly what you don't want her to feel. She feels like you are pushing her boundaries. Here are some things that you should never say or do.

* Engaging in sex conversations with unrequited partners.

* Sharing inappropriate images or jokes together.

* Absolute disregard for her physical borders.

These are just three ways you can make a woman feel uncomfortable. Women have to deal with this type of man many times in their lifetime. You can end all chances of having a good relationship with her.

When to Approach

This is a problem that many men struggle with. To avoid coming across as creepy or threatening, men tend to avoid women. This can be frightening for women. You can meet and talk to anyone if you do not find it strange. It is the only way humans interact and get along with each other. However, there's a time and place where you can and cannot approach a lady. Allow your instincts and judgements to guide you in such situations. Here are some things you should keep in your mind.

Locate

If you do not intend to appear creepy, even accidentally, the first thing to consider is the setting. You might approach a woman in a sunny park, but not in a darkly lit alleyway while she is walking home at evening. In some cases, like bars and clubs, people are expecting to be approached with the opposite kind of sex. These places are not for women, and they may find it disturbing if someone approaches them in the darkness. It's important to be aware of where you are and what the occasion is. At a funeral, flirting with someone is frowned upon. But, at a wedding, this is possible.

Never Leave Her Behind

When approaching a woman, keep these points in mind. However you should not make her feel restricted or trapped. Always be mindful of how you approach her. Talking to a woman in a beach setting is quite normal. If you approach the same woman at the motel's laundromat, or in a hotel laundry, it can be quite threatening. Even if it isn't your intention to confront her, blocking the exit or the doorway with your body will seem to be threatening. These are all simple rules to keep in mind when approaching a woman. Just be aware of your surroundings and the circumstances.

Respect Her Privacy

If you find yourself questioning whether it is appropriate for you to approach a woman while you talk, it is a smart idea to keep a safe distance. If she allows you to, do not intrude into her space. As stated earlier, make it a habit to allow her to have free access and space to go where she pleases.

Conversational Strategies

We are constantly told repeatedly that Mars is the home of men and Venus the home for women. Most people think that men and women are opposed and don't have much to share. Here are some tips that will help you have a pleasant and productive conversation with women.

Looking Beyond the Facade

All of us are skin and bones. We all have unique personalities under our clothes. Everyone has baggage, and each of us can be haunted by our past. You don't have all those things haunting you. People don't like to be reminded about past events or negative aspects of their lives. You must be able see through the woman's facade when you speak to her. You need to take the time to get her to open up and understand her. Whatever your background, it is important to have a real connection with her before you try to chat.

Building Common Ground

To build understanding, you should take the time to identify common points. This skill can be useful in all areas of your life that you need to interact. You could, for example, go to a grocery store or other places where you can interact with others. You can find out something about the checkout staff when you reach the counter. Personal experience has shown that women often spend a lot more time and effort dressing up. When you notice someone wearing nice accessories, compliment her. This will immediately make the other person look at you and respond to your compliments.

Let Her Talk

This is an easy task. You don't need to appear brilliant or incredible. Just be a good listener, and let her speak. Be attentive and not distracted while listening to her. Keep your responses to the subject in mind. It's as easy as that. You might have complimented a woman's accessory in the example above, which opened the door to a conversation. She may share some information about the accessory such as, "I bought this for my birthday!". You can then use this opportunity to tell her something she will like. You don't want to start talking about yourself. Be clear that you are trying get her to speak to you. It's easy to learn this trick after a few attempts.

Avoid Certain Topics

You should avoid all subjects that may cause disagreement. To make someone dislike you, the simplest way to do it is to take a different view than theirs and tell them you are wrong. Let's suppose that the woman we used as an example agreed to go with you for a cup o' coffee. This is an important step. So, congratulations! You don't have to impress her by being smart or strong. If you do this, your last date will be over the cup of coffee you share. Instead, you should find topics that both of you can talk about.

I would suggest you to avoid politics if you don't agree on it. Until you feel comfortable with each others opinions, You should avoid any topics that spark passion or strong opinions. Avoid sexy and unwholesome topics. Avoid any topics that may cause a heated discussion. Remember that both you and she have the right of opinion. But, the goal is to communicate with her. A disagreement will destroy any chance that you might have.

Don't invade her private space

Respect her space. Don't get too close and don't try blocking her body. Keep an arm's reach between you and her. You can speak to her by leaning towards her, but not in her private space.

Personal Hygiene Is Important

Before you approach a woman, brush your teeth. Bad breath can make a conversation end much quicker than other things. You can stop the conversation by having a cup o coffee, or smoking before you begin to chew on breath mints. You should always have some mints with your wherever you go. You must take care of your hygiene. Your appearance is as important as how you present yourself.

Chapter 13: Amazing Scientific Theory Regarding Dating

Let us now talk about the scientific theories that men love to talk about when trying to get a girl. You'll find many amazing scientific theories related to dating in dating books and pick up manuals that were written by numerous experts. While some of these theories may be true, the majority of them are based upon lies. Yes, they boast of a scientific theory without any credible evidence. Unfortunately, we are often swayed by their lies all the time.

This chapter will show you how to make sure you have a successful first date. This chapter will give information about theories and their limitations, as well the reasons they are not useful.

As I mentioned in the preceding chapter, the peacocking theory was completely false. This is because men often wear expensive clothing to the bar and disco. You will always see someone wearing brighter and more expensive clothes than you.

Let's discredit some of those scientific theories you see online. One example is seduction via the use of magic words. A number of websites offer premium advice, which is based in NLP or persuading techniques that can subconsciously affect your target. Actually, hypnotizing your target to get them to do the things you want is completely stupid. Even if there are magical words you can share with your date, they will never listen. Hypnosis doesn't work. It is a low-cost trick that people use to extract money.

You'll hear a lot of magic pills and sprays online that can improve your game. Sprays that are advertised online often contain pheromones. They signal chemicals that increase the libido levels of women who sniff them. Many pheromones sold online are often made of a mixture of perfume and water. Some are even from the testicles or lions' baboons. Magic pills can be either sugar pills or dangerously mated narcotics, which are illegal in several countries.

Finally, there is the negation principle. The theory holds that the more you make women feel insulted or give her negative suggestions, the greater her chances of her lowering her defenses and eventually accepting you into her lives. Examples of negative suggestions you can make to women are: how normal they dress, how simple their clothes are, how small their bodies are, how little they talk, and how loud they speak. This theory can be offensive and even ruin your chances.

So why is the negation thesis a fallacy. Women are emotional. They are likely to feel sorry for themselves and will be easily offended if you give negative feedback. Instead of getting your attention, they may pour their drink all over you. They might call the bouncers at the club to throw you out. This is why negation theory isn't a good way to pick up women.

Chapter 14: Game Time

Now that your profiles have been set up, it's time for you to move forward. Zig Ziglar once said that to be a winning person, you have to plan to win. Prepare to win. And expect to win. This book provides enough information to make you a winner in the online dating game. You can learn something from every interaction. Let's get ready! Let's go, friend!

Bumble App

Here are some of the things that I do with Bumble. Like I mentioned earlier, you have unlimited swipes. So I encourage you to swipe every chance that you get. I want to add that I don't glance at profiles when I swipe left. This is because it takes time to view every profile and image. But, since Bumble offers unlimited swipes, I always swipe to right on ALL PROFILES! It's not easy to go through every profile and pick the best ones. If women respond to me and are interested in me, I will reply and let her know. If she's not my kind, I will simply ignore her message.

My first time using Bumble I used to spend too much time looking at profiles before I would swipe left or back. I now swipe right for all profiles. Bumble allows me the freedom to swipe anywhere I want, however I prefer the evening hours because Bumble uses location-based technology so I know that women will be home at night.

I swipe while I wait in line or waiting for someone, or in church. You get my point. It's a numbers-based game. My first experience with Bumble was not successful. It took me a few months before I found someone. Then it was easy to find the right person. As I said earlier, when something happens in the "universe", you start attracting all these ladies and you go zero to multiple women messaging. It's the frequency of your vibration. It's my belief or theory. This is how it works. I should also mention that I enjoy dating multiple females. I swipe right on every single profile because of this. At the moment, I don't want to be in a monogamous marriage, but I will soon. You can still use the principles in this book for any kind of relationship or marriage.

Tinder App

Tinder is fast and easy to setup. I prefer to swipe Monday to Friday after 6pm. It's location-based like Bumble. This means that I want the women in my vicinity to be home when the swipes are made. I always look at the pictures before I swipe right or left, unlike Bumble. You can only swipe 100 times. (Swiping to the left when someone isn't your favorite doesn't count toward your 100 "Likes" swipes.) It's best that you only swipe for women you like. I swipe anytime of the day, except on weekends. I use the free version and it has been great for me. That is why I am cautious with my swipes.

If you're not averse to the paid membership, then sign-up for the unlimited swipes. I'd also change my strategy and use all my 100 "likeswipes". I'll do this by switching my strategy to use my 100 likes every 12 hour. So, for example, I'd swipe all my 100 likes at either 7 or 8 am, or 7 or 8 pm, then again at 7 or 8. To swipe again, the free version must be used within 12 hours of using up your 100 like-swipes. This is a great way to speed up the process. Tinder works great for me even though there seem to have been a lot more women of lower quality on it, these days. That's why I don't like it as much. However, this might not be the case in your area.

Ok-Cupid (OKC)

Another of my favorite sites is Ok-Cupid. While it is more traditional in online dating, you can also swipe on women who are interested. Unfortunately, both men and women will not be able see the other person who liked you. This feature is not as popular but still works. If women with the upgraded version notice that you liked them they will match up with you. Similar to the other two dating apps. Keep it simple. Fill in your "About Me" section. Click on any of the categories that apply to you. Now you are ready to start messaging these women. I don't read their profile. I might scan it if the length is too short. But I mostly look at the pictures. If she looks attractive enough to me, then I'll send them a simple message. (If you have the time, take the time and read her profile. If she is interested, leave a comment, ask any questions or share some humor.

Only after she sends me a message, will I read her profile. You don't want spend too much time going through profiles to find "The One". After spending half of the day thinking about what message you want to send, you finally have the message you are looking for. You hit the send button nervously and guess who? You don't get a reply! It can be mentally draining to send elaborate messages. I can understand why some men give up online dating. I have sent a few messages and received no replies. It can be exhausting and discouraging. But, I am here and I will make it work. This book is meant to maximize your results while not mentally draining you.

I encourage you to message all women that are your type, and any woman that you find attractive, even if they seem out of your league. Do not worry if she is younger or older than yours, as long her legal age is met, she can message you. It will surprise you at the things that happen! You'll be surprised at what happens! There are beautiful, easy-going women out there. If you message the right people, you can get them on your side and start dating. There are many beautiful women out there that are good-looking and are happy to be sexy! Don't let this shit go to you! She will miss her chance to get to know an amazing man like you. There are many women who aren't as attractive as you and behave like bitches. I do not entertain that type of behavior. I don't have the time and you shouldn't either.

Sending the first message is a good idea. Don't exaggerate her ego. Examples of what not to use are: "Hey, sexy", and "Hey pretty", as well as "Hey hot girl", "Damn! You're so hot", and "Wow, you're gorgeous!" You get the idea! What I love to say is, "Hey young woman", "Hey sweetheart", "Hey beautiful lady"," "Hey dear", etc. You can also add a personal message. The idea is to create a neutral term or phrase that portrays her personality. It can be used for any woman, old, young, or ugly. The words are not important as regards to attractiveness. You can still use them towards your grandmother LOL. This method works well, as it makes your message stand out among all the other "Hey Beautiful", "Hey sexy", and other messages she receives. I'm not saying "Hey beautiful" and "Hey sexy messages don't work. However, they aren't nearly as effective now as they were in years past. They worked for me many times but they were less effective over time. It might work for your business.

Get her Number

Try to identify commonalities as soon you start to speak to her. Maybe you like the same artist, enjoy the same cuisine, have a common hobby, or share a similar love for something. Don't lose this little bit of information. You can mention this later on in the conversation. If she mentions that she likes Mexican food, you can tell her that you know the address of a small Mexican restaurant she would love to visit. It is easy to ask her for her number.

Once you have the number you need, you can begin messaging her. Start a casual conversation with her. You will see how she responds. If she replies quickly and attempts to continue the discussion, you have her green signal. Be sure to not send inappropriate messages and don't text too often.

Let me end with a final tip: If she does not feel interested in you then it is time to move on. If she signals to your in any way that she isn't interested in continuing the conversation then it is time you say goodbye. Even though you may be a lovely person, if she isn't interested in you continuing the conversation, it is time for you to look for someone else. You shouldn't let one rejection devastate your self-confidence.

You can have easy conversations with women if you keep these simple tips in view. But you'll need to practice this a few more times until you feel confident.

Chapter 15: First Steal Their Hearts, Then Conquer Their Souls

"There's a time in a journey when something sweet, as irresistible or charming as wine, wells up inside the traveller."

-Patrick MacGill

Men will try to conquer women's hearts at every chance. They try to charm women, but sometimes that doesn't work. This is not their fault. They have never learned how to charm women. It is an integral part in picking up women. However, it takes effort from the man.

You must show her that you value your personality and are worth keeping. Women want a committed, independent, and focused man for a long-term marriage. A woman wouldn't want to be in a long-term relationship with a non-serious or clumsy father-child.

You need to be attractive to women to make yourself irresistible. Here are some qualities that will help you to become the best version you can be. You should be cautious and not try to sell yourself. If you try to make yourself a star and compare your partner's wealth and status, this can be a major turnoff for women. You don't need to be wealthy or famous to attract women. If you want to have a serious relationship with someone, it is not worth the effort.

Charismatic behavior that is not physically based can be hard. Men may have to adapt parts of themselves. Don't worry. It will be a positive change that will make your life better, even if things don't go according to plan.

Here are some secrets to making yourself irresistible

Attracting women is not an easy task. It takes effort and determination to make a difference. These hacks will make it easy for you to look like the perfect woman.

* Women Like Leaders

Women will be attracted to a man who is capable of taking control of situations. Men who can lead and guide others, acting as role models, will often be successful in relationships. This is because they are practical and can understand what sacrifices and efforts are necessary.

Be sure to not become a dictator. Don't assume control over a situation. You don't have the right to make decisions for your girl. Women dislike being controlled by men. Let her have her freedom and space. Do not try to make her live a dictatorship because of something you read.

If you are leading a couple, it is important to talk to her first about how your relationship is progressing and what you hope for in the future. She might not agree with your views, but she will be grateful that you decided to express your feelings and not wait for her to do so. This can even work in your favor if you had previously doubts about her casual dating.

* Women Love Reliability & Selflessness

Women love men who are trustworthy and reliable. You should not make her doubt you intentions. While you may be making jokes about them, she will have multiple red flags that will warn her to stop talking about them.

Be sure to make her needs your first priority. Even if your talk stage is only the beginning, make sure to keep her needs and desires at the forefront. Let her know she is important to you. If she can see that you're a reliable, selfless man, then you will become more attractive.

* Women love good listeners

What do women love to do most? Talk. Ask her what she would like you to do. Listen to her. Although she might be telling you about some random thing, such as a new employee at her workplace or a new dress, you should listen to her and not drift off to your lunch.

Get to know her by talking with her. Show her how much you care about her life by being attentive. Be sure to tell her.

* Women Love Thoughtful Men

Many ways you can show thoughtfulness are possible. It is possible to be thoughtful in many different ways. It'd be a great thing if you shared your feelings with her.

A lot of compassion can go a long way. Never forget to thank her for your kindness. If you're out for dinner with her, show kindness to waiters, tip well, and treat them with respect. Be kind to your friends and spend quality time with your loved ones. Always be respectful to women and act like you're a gentleman. These will make your girl more attracted to you.

* Women Love Well-Managed Men

While you may be a good guy in most aspects, you can have a negative temperament that makes it difficult to get along with others. You shouldn't be rude to your girl or anyone for that matter. Your manners are a reflection of how you were raised.

A man who is angry and uses a harsh tone will instantly shut down a woman. It doesn't matter if this is your first time speaking to her. It will be free and she will love it.

* Women Love Humorous Men

Do you manage to make her laugh. Is she going to roar with laughter at your jokes, or is she already laughing? If the answer is yes, then you are already in good standing with her. Girls love guys who make them laugh.

You shouldn't also joke too often. There are limits on humor. Also, not every joke is funny. Jokes that make women laugh or are insensitive will not go down well. She'd be furious if you laughed about something that shouldn't be. Men who make unnecessary jokes aren't liked by women because it shows that they don't take any seriousness.

Your sense of humor is a gift. Knowing when to use a joke is an art.

The Secret to a Woman's Heart

* Look Confident

Confidence is vital, as I have repeatedly stated. Confidence is key if your goal is to win women's hearts. Make sure you are confident about yourself and what it is that you want. Unsimplified men can be a problem.

Believe in yourself. Be confident in your ability to please women. Keep believing that the woman whom you are chasing will be yours. Your self-worth and worthiness will be reflected in her.

* Surprise Her

You don't have to do a lot to show your appreciation for women. However, this is false. You don't have a need to take her on a cruise just to show your affection. Small gestures can make women feel happy and bring you adoration. Send her a note or take your chair at a restaurant. These small gestures can seem trivial, but they will bring joy to her heart.

* Claim Her

Don't be controlling, but let her know you are there for her. Possessiveness is a good thing. But don't let it become toxic. Do your best to take care of her. Give her a shoulder to cry on when she is unhappy and share in her joy. All a woman desires from a husband is for him to be willing to try. You must defend your woman against anyone who would disrespect her and you must take care. You will receive back what your give and she will find you irresistible.

Experts on love, relationship and marriage have found that it's easy to win women's hearts. Make an effort to be the kind woman women love.

* Be Pursuant

Chase her. While a woman is attracted to being pursued, it's not a good idea to put pressure on her. Let her make that decision for herself, but let her know you are interested in more.

* Be a Gentleman

Don't be rude or arrogant. Respect her and show kindness when you go out. She can be the one to open the car doors, take her to a restaurant and let her order. These ideas may seem old-fashioned, but they still work.

* Romance can go a long way

You shouldn't let romance die. It doesn't matter if you aren't in a romantic relationship yet. You just need to be romantic. You can start by being romantic but not too intense. The way you interact with her and your behavior around her should be enough to show her how much you love her.

* Clear Your Intentions

Let her know what you are looking to accomplish. Invite her along to your games nights and parties. She will be delighted and feel that you want her to meet new friends.

* Be yourself

Women are excellent at detecting fakeness. Don't lie to her. And don't pretend you're someone else. Women can easily tell if your confidence is faked to approach her. Be yourself and you will have an advantage over men who make it look too easy. If you're not trying to be something she doesn't like, she will love you more.

Your personality is probably the most important thing about you. While you may need to work on your courting skills, these tips can help. It all comes down to how you use the tips to make yourself attractive to women.

Chapter 16: Concrete Examples For A Perfect Date

Dates based upon Learning and Socializing

You will introduce her new people to her and will show her something you don't know. A woman who is social and has lots of friends and acquaintances will be very attracted to a sociable man. You will find that you are open to learning new things and can be patient with others. This type of date is very attractive.

Here are some logistical ways to do it.

1. She came to you because she agreed to take a course with you.

2. Make a quick stop at a store to ask questions, buy things or greet friends as you head towards the course.

3. Keep the course straight and learn from it.

4. Take aperitifs in a local restaurant where you have a good relationship with the staff.

5. Take a walk along a street or square.

6. If you want to end the date at home, invite your friend to visit.

Fashion and Culture are the basis of date

By attending this event, she will see that you are capable to look after yourself.

1. You were both shopping and you met at the centre.

2. Explain to the staff that you are located in that building.

3. You want to purchase an accessory for yourself (bracelet. scarf. necklace. hat. etc.). Ask her for an opinion.

4. Shop for what you want;

5. You stop by the bookstore to find out if it has the book that you ordered or to visit a friend.

6. You can go together for a coffee or ice-cream.

7. Invite her in to your house. Inviting her to visit, close by your house.

Dates based in Sport and Nature

By this date, it is clear that you care about your health. It will be attractive for women to see a man who values his physical condition, his well being and the environment.

1. You have agreed and agreed to play volleyball, a race, or other sporting activity.

2. You can buy food and drink at a supermarket.

3. Relax by going for a walk through the nearby park.

4. Go past your old workplace/home/school;

5. Take a break at the bar you love and enjoy a cup of coffee.

6. You know what to expect.

It's much easier than you thought.

Pick two main themes that are most important to you and mix them well.

The last example shows you where to take her, with fewer "steps". In the next chapters, you will learn what to say as well as what to do.

Dates based primarily on Art and Animals

Your participation in this event will prove that you have the ability to show empathy and care for others. She will be impressed by your empathy and sensitivity.

1. You have agreed not to miss an exhibition or other event.

2. Take a long walk and find a place to sit on a stool. It is possible to take your dog along to a park, where they can run free of charge. Or, you can simply stop by the nearest pet shop to watch the kittens. You can pretend that the place you pick is divided into multiple places. You can use it as a park entrance, a bench and a fountain. A park area could also be used as a court area, parking area, playground or skatepark. As though they were many different places. Similar results can be achieved for large bookstores or shopping centres.

You can modify the order in which she is taken to suit your needs.

You have so many options!

What do you think? What is easier? A galant dinner with expectations can create pressure, discomfort, embarrassing silences and uncomfortable silences. Or are you more comfortable talking to a woman if you're at ease in familiar surroundings?

You will have the luxury of having all the time in this world to dine with her.

Chapter 17: From Dating To Relating

Communicating effectively is difficult enough. Communicating effectively in a couple can be even more challenging. When communication is impeded, couples often have the worst problems. Long-term relationships are more difficult. You would expect communication to be easy with someone you so love and care for. But that's not always true. It can happen more often than you think. You will have to struggle to communicate with your man. Communication breakdowns can lead to a couple feeling more distant and frustrated than they used to be. You might find it difficult to communicate when you are having arguments that become so frequent you don't know your partner anymore.

If communication is so hard, how are you supposed relate to the man.

You can always remind yourself of this basic fact. Women need different things to feel loved and fulfilled in relationships than men. True, men have their needs and wants. However, because they have been taught from an early age to keep their vulnerabilities and feelings hidden, they often suppress them. Instead, men must challenge their will to succeed and work with others to get ahead. Men are conditioned to deny or suppress their vulnerable side. This side is part of all of us. Men are also vulnerable.

Men put on a brave front in the same way that a "real man" should. We forget that they are creatures with another side. He was a boy who displayed qualities such as being fearless, independent, ambitious, driven, responsible, and driven by goals. As he grew up, however, these qualities made him appear insensitive and harsh. He is not learning the "how to be man" lessons that were given to boys, and they don't promote or encourage any type of learning or development. If he continued to behave the same way and displayed the same personality traits which made others think he had been a brave little man for speaking up when he grew up, he will be seen by women as closed-off, indifferent, or someone difficult to relate too.

This conditioned men to suppress their emotions, and instead choose to stay task-oriented, only focusing on what was necessary. This unfortunately leads to many problems in his intimate and romantic relationships. He may work too hard and not pay enough attention, which can lead to her believing he doesn't really care for her. She begins to feel disillusioned and lost. Soon the relationship will be overthrown. For a man to feel connected with her on a deeper level, he must understand the woman.

You need to spend time together doing what you love to be able to relate to a guy. Find out about his interests and passions. He will be excited to share these things with you. Spend more time doing activities you both enjoy. Spending quality time together will strengthen your relationship. Try hiking, long walks, volunteering, and, if you are feeling adventurous, trying out different activities so that you can share the joy of doing something new. Find something you enjoy together. It will allow you to explore other common interests.

It is important to show your man kindness, compassion, affection. Couples often forget this aspect after being comfortable in their relationship for a while and feel that sex is sufficient intimacy. Men need to remind themselves that they have a loving and supportive partner in their relationship. They are someone who cares about them. Simple gestures such holding his hand as you walk or talk to him, placing your head on the shoulders of his back when you're side-by-side, and giving him a quick peck on his cheek. Get him his favorite coffee and surprise him with his favorite breakfast. You can also pick up his favorite snack items during your grocery shop run. These small moments that only lovers can share are how to better connect with your man.

Happy Couples: The Habits

Happy couples work hard together, but they also have certain routines and habits that keep them happy. Here are some habits that happy couples share that help them keep a smile on their faces.

They have a shared routine - Happy couples will make it a habit to share one or more rituals. It could be sharing the chores of brushing teeth together, cooking together, or even doing the dishes together.

* Going to Bed Together- A happy couple will make it a daily habit to get up at the same hour every night. In the beginning, it was exciting to go to bed together. Comfortingly, falling asleep next to your loved one is a comforting experience. Happily married couples continue to do this routine as often as they can.

* Show Generosity with Complements - A happy couple will never stop complimenting their partner. It keeps the love alive.

* They Create Shared Interests. Happy couples will find common interests to be involved in. They cultivated shared interests they didn't have before.

* Hug your partner - Happy couples make it an habit to hug one another for several minutes every morning. You can do it

every morning as you wake up, before going to bed at night when you return home, and whenever you feel like a cuddle. Warm embraces from the one you love are the best comforting feelings in this world.

They Hold Hands. - They are walking side by sides if they're not holding hands. This is how happy and healthy couples are able to enjoy each other's company. They remain close even when they're away from each other.

* They Kiss Before They Leave - A happy couple will kiss their partner goodbye as a way to say "I love you" and wish them a great day.

* They Make Forgiveness, Trust, and Respect a Priority. This is the one habit that happy couples put a lot of importance on. It's making forgiveness and trust a key mode of operation. They quickly forgive

each others when they disagree. They trust each others to be the support system that they need. Their partners are also trustworthy enough to not feel suspicious of their partner's company when they're around other people.

They Keep Their Eyes on the Good Things. Every relationship has its good and bad moments, but happy couples are different from other couples in that they tend to focus on the positives more than the negatives. They know that the bad times won't last so they don't have to be dreadful. The good times are what they cherish for the rest of their lives.

They don't nag and nitpick. Happy couples do not nag or nitpick on their partner. They know that this isn't the way to warm someones heart and instead they choose to talk about it.

* They Say, "I Love You Every Day" - If you love someone, it is important that you tell them every day. This is one thing happy couples do daily to remind each other that there are people who love them. A great way to set the mood for a positive day is to hug your partner and tell them you love him before you go. The moment you hear you are loved, it makes you feel so happy.

* They Wish Each other a Great day - While every day presents its challenges, happy couples make each other's day brighter by setting a positive attitude to start their day. You can simply wish your partner good health and a bright day. This will help them get out of bed with a smile on the face, make their mornings more enjoyable, and keep them smiling no matter what.

Good Morning and Good Night. They say good morning to each other every morning, and goodnight at night. Even if there has been an argument or how they feel about it, happy couples who make it a point not to say sorry to their partner are showing that they still love each other despite the difficulties.

They make their own fun. When life feels a little bit too routine and monotonous, happy couples will go out to create their own entertainment by breaking from the norm every now and then. Happy couples share a genuine love for each other, which is why their relationship flourishes even when the rest of society fails. They're open to having fun, and they will sometimes break the rules if they have to.

* Check In With Them – Happy couples check in daily to see how the day is going. If their partner is having trouble, they cheer them up. They can share in their partner's joy when they are having a good day. It is these small gestures that remind one another how much you care.

* They're proud to be with their partners - Happy couple are proud to be together. They don't have to feel ashamed or embarrassed and they won't be competing against other strangers to be the most attractive partner. They only care about being with someone who makes their lives better.

* No Phone Policy- Happy couples have a no-phone policy. This is one of the best ways to keep your relationship happy. They make it an effort to be there for their partner when they're together. The rest, such as responding to email or browsing social media, can wait until their bonding time. This is a common sight to see couples dining out but instead of talking, scrolling through social media and becoming more interested in what's happening than actually enjoying each other.

Chapter 18: Picking The Date

Now you are ready to meet the right guy or girl. Many advances have been made in the world of dating. There are many options available to help you find the right date. People nowadays are seeking out variety and diversity. There are several options: speed dating; blind dating; casual dating; double dating; and many more.

Speed dating is often organized by a specific dating company. Before the event begins, participants must register. They go to a venue, which could be a bar or restaurant, and meet other dating candidates. Typically, the interaction lasts 5-10 minutes. This type of date relies heavily upon first impressions. Candidates can also meet more candidates to determine which one is most compatible.

Speed dating is great for those who are looking to improve their social and communication skills. Speed dating is great for people who are comfortable meeting strangers but don't bother to strike up a conversation. If you are an introvert, you will not find this kind of dating appealing.

Online dating is where people meet over the internet. The cyber world allows the two parties to meet and get to know their other. The 21st-century way of dating has been made possible by many dating apps. This is great for couples who live in different cities, or even from different countries. But once the connection is established and is already strong, both parties will eventually meet to explore a more serious relationship.

People today prefer online dating, especially those who are always in motion. It is easy to set up and takes less time than other dating options. Because you can see the screen in front, it is an excellent way to protect yourself from striking up a genuine conversation. But, this method of dating can also be very dangerous as you cannot know for certain who the person is behind the screen. Some people are dishonest in what they say. Be careful.

Blind dating refers to when two people do not know one another but are introduced by close friends, family members or coworkers in order to set up a date. They serve as the matchmaker for the two parties. You don't usually know each other's looks, so it is called a 'blind' date. Sometimes, however the matchmaker may give both of you a general idea about the other such as their physical bodies and common interests.

Blind dating is ideal for adventurous thrill-seekers. This adds excitement to dating. Blind dates are a common way for love at first glance. You never know who your love story is. Blind dates should not be a reason to hate someone because they do not meet your expectations, at least not physically.

Casual dating can be when one is able to date many people. It could be one-sided or can include both of the parties. This type is best for those who aren't looking to make a commitment and/or make a promise. People who are into casual dating tend to think that they should'see what the rest of the world can offer me' before settling down with the one or two that they do find. Or, worse, for people who do not want to settle down.

But you need to be cautious when entering into such a relationship. Most people mistake casual dating for casual sex. It is important to be open to a relationship without too many emotions or none. The moment you develop feelings for your partner, you may want more. You will feel lucky if you and your date feel the same. It will be a shame if he/she does not.

Double dating means two people going out together. This is common in younger dating scenes. This type allows both the partners to interact with each other, which keeps the conversation moving. This date is often chosen when either one of the couples has just begun to have a conversation. This allows them to avoid situations where the conversation becomes dry. You can also see how your date interacts to other people.

Double dates are often between close friends. This is because your best friend will get to meet your date, and vice versa. You will also feel more comfortable and at ease. But make sure everyone can get along because clashing personalities are not a good idea. That is not good for both you and your date. Not because you were at fault, but because your friend was with your date. This can be even more tragic and depressing, so be aware.

Your standards will help you choose the best type of dating to meet your 'right one. You will find the perfect match for you if these tips are taken into consideration. Remember, success is only possible when you plan it well.

Chapter 19: Stop Behaving Like A Weak Men

Women are attracted not to weakness, but strength. Your masculine strength can make a woman desire to be in a relationship with you. A strong man is someone a woman seeks.

It can ruin the attraction if you feel like a woman is controlling you or pushing you around. "Bad guys" make women turn on them because they have dominant qualities. "Nice guys," however, are the opposite.

I was a super nice guy when I first met my wife. She said she didn't trust him. I am always open and honest with you," I thought to myself. "How is it possible that she doesn't trust me?"

I learned why she said that when I started investing in dating and relationships. I was always available and doing her will, but I was indirect and cautious in my approach. I failed to be strong enough and was sometimes pushed aside by her.

Because she didn't trust me, she started to doubt my masculine power. As you probably know, women who don't trust men can't romantically fall in love with them. My weaknesses were a constant test for her. She also found me flakey. Women will judge you based on your weaknesses and make you appear weaker.

A woman who senses weakness will start testing you more frequently. Tests of a man's strength are an automatic response. Multiple women have done the same thing to me. This is why it is so important to understand what she is asking you. She will be more attracted if your pass her test but she will be disappointed if it fails. It's worth noting, however, that the more you love her, the less likely she is to test you.

7.1. Women test men

Below are some examples from tests women use for determining if a woman is an emotional strong person or a caregiver.

The message testing

You can expect her to take several hours to reply to your messages. She is trying to gauge how you will respond. Her attraction to you will decrease if you react in a negative way. Sending her a message in a second response only makes the situation worse and makes her want more.

You should wait for the reply from a woman before sending another message. Some men send a message to a woman and, when they don't get a reply, insult and slander her. Such responses will lead to nothing and only reinforce the fact that she knows better: that turning down you is the right choice for her.

The no call test

When she promises she will call you, but does not follow through as promised she is testing you. In order to gauge your reaction, some women intentionally do this. If she claims she will call you, wait until she actually calls. If you try to call her back again, she will reject you. It is not attractive to be needy.

The "I can control" test

She will test you if she sees you are busy, but she still asks you to do something.

I vividly recall the day that I was working in my office when the woman I was currently dating sent me a text message asking me to assist her with the photocopy machine. I ran to help her. Can you guess what happened next? Her surprise at my quick arrival was surprising. She told me that she was impressed by my quick arrival.

I left what was going on and went to help her. It ruined the attraction that she felt towards me. It was an indication that she could control and manipulate me, which is not very masculine.

You shouldn't refuse to help a girl you are in a relationship if she asks. But, you should ensure that her request is legitimate. In my instance, the way she requested help was incorrect. She sat in her own office and sent me an SMS requesting that I help her with her photocopier machine. If I had the knowledge now, I would have stood by my conviction and said "I would love to help but I am too busy with work." If it is urgent I can do it later after I finish my current project.

This response would have made her more respectful of me. But, since I was an eager-toplease servant in that instance her attraction towards me dropped. She even admitted that she had just arrived quickly.

It is your responsibility as a man to make sure that your lady knows that you will not tolerate second-class treatment. It is important that your woman knows that you will not accept second-class treatment. If you allow a woman to walk all over your body and you do not take action, it is a sign that you are failing as an individual man.

If a woman you desire is controlling or manipulative, walk away. It will show her that you understand your worth and that it is important to you that you love and appreciate yourself. It is not possible to be a passive observer of someone pushing you around, as if you were a nobody. If you're treating a woman respectably and loving her, but she isn't reciprocating, get out of her way as soon as possible and find someone who will.

Remember: always demonstrate a masculine vibe. For women, humor, masculinity, confidence and masculinity are all attractive. Masculine energy involves drive, purpose and mission. It also helps to break down barriers, achieve goals, and overcome them. It is direct and decisive as well as fearless. Women are drawn to men who will pursue what they desire, regardless of their failure potential and fears.

Even if she rejects, a woman is more likely to respect you if you are willing to go on a first date or if you get to the point quickly and set up a date.

A commitment to success in all areas of life is essential. It must be unaffected or discouraged by failures and rejections. Similar to dating, it is a process that involves getting through the Nos to reach the Yeses.

Chapter 20: The First Meet-Up

It's now time to meet up in person! To start, I will say, never suggest that we meet up for dinner or go on the first meetup. It's expensive and will result in you spending more money if you have multiple dates with the same woman. First meetups are a chance to meet up over drinks, coffee/tea and healthy smoothies. I will pay for the first drink. She will then pay for the next round. If the date went well but we had only one drink, I will tell her "I'll make this payment, you'll pay the next time." We'll split the bill if we don't have a good time. I never open a bar tab. I only pay for the drinks I order. You can meet her at a coffee shop. She will order your food separately and you can pay individually. Note also that I refer the first encounter as a meeting up, not a date. You should never refer it to as a date to the woman. Some women may be scared of this because it places too much pressure on them to use the term "date".

Once you have her consent to meet you in-person, you want to be able to suggest a location that she will feel at ease in. Men, take the initiative and recommend a few places to her. Unconfident, weak men who are unable to decide for themselves and don't have the courage to research a few locations can make women turn away. Never ask her to recommend a location where you can meet. You can ask her to suggest a location, but don't immediately agree. Let her know that you will check it out and let her if it is good. Do not worry if you don't know anything about the area you'll be meeting in. You can visit "Google Maps" to see the street view of the area and then check it out. You can also search for other places to meet her on google maps, including bars, lounges and coffee shops. I like to keep my distance settings on my dating profiles to a minimum of 10 miles. I used to set it to 50 miles at one time, but that became overwhelming because so many women were messaging me. I'm very picky now and I have my filters in place. I only care about women I like within my geographic distance. (You will also get to that point!) For women who are interested in my interests. It's better because I have my favorite places that I want to meet women for the first-time.

There are places that offer drinks with relaxing music and live bands depending on the week. I also have lounges with fire pits, coffee shops, books with coffee shops, and coffee shops that have couches. While I love to recommend places nearby, I don't always mention my location until after we meet up. Only if we find it interesting, however. I would invite them over to my place. There would be no pressure. We would continue drinking, listening to music, or doing something more relaxing. Sometimes we end up having some sex or just sitting on my sofa having a good discussion. I always try to get there earlier than she does to look around and grab some seats. If she is arriving, give her a warm hug. It is a comforting gesture to extend your hand to her and give her a hug. Some men only shake her hand to make it seem like a business meeting. Then they give her a hug at the end and try to get physical. This can make her feel uncomfortable, especially if you don't feel any connection. Men should keep eye contact with their date, smile, lean forward, and make hand gestures while sharing stories. If done correctly, it will increase comfort.

Keep good eye contact. Try to look into her soul with a soft gaze. If necessary, you can break eye contact. Some men may give her a blank stare, making her feel uncomfortable. It's fine to scan the room. In my next book I'll cover more about the power and importance of eye contact. It is a gesture to the woman that you are putting your face in front of the door. This means she is giving up control and she can relax. Always be prepared to signal the waiters, request the check and keep an eye out for any "danger" at the door. Since childhood, this was how I was taught. While I do not know who invented this crap, it is something that many women are aware of. This is a great way to boost your odds of success. Keep in mind, you must be the man you claim to be. Women enjoy a man controlling them.

Please Wear Your Best for The Meet Up

These are my suggestions for clothes to wear to your first meetup. Think semi-casual. You could wear polos or casual button-downs. Or, you could choose a nice fitted tee or sweater depending on the weather. Regular fit clothing will also work if you don't love fitted clothing. My personal preference is to wear any color polo shirts, fitted jeans, or loafers, but I prefer darker colors. I also have a watch on my left hand and a bracelet for my right. Make sure your men brush their teeth to prevent bad breath! Breath mints are a good idea to have on hand in case of emergency. Bad breath is a huge turn off for women. Bad breath can make me feel irritated, no matter how beautiful she may be.

I will trim or shave my beard. I use cologne on my neck, body and chest before I put on my shirt. I prefer to do this after I have had a shower. After a hot bath, your pores will expand, trapping the scent of your cologne and keeping you smelling good for longer. Apply cologne only to clean, dry skin. I don't think anyone wants to feel like they are in a gym locker room with the scent of their cologne. Men, iron your clothes and make sure they are properly pressed. It is common for men to not iron their clothes when they get home from work. Some men will meet up with women while they're still dressed in work clothes, it's okay as long as your line of work doesn't require you to get dirty just make sure you freshen up a bit, but if you have a laborious job (construction-worker, auto-mechanic, maintenance, etc.) It's okay for men to meet women while they are still wearing work clothes. However, if you have a laborious job (construction-worker, auto-mechanic, maintenance), please shower and change.

If you're unable to shower or change clothes due to illness, make sure to get yourself ready and dressed in the most professional manner. It is vital that you notify her by texting, calling, or calling her. This will let her know that your meeting will take place after work. I was once on a first date with one the women I was seeing and she shared some of her worst experiences. One of those dates was about a guy she met online. They were getting drinks at a club for the first time. This man worked for a construction firm and arrived at the lounge dressed in work clothes and boots. She claimed that his clothes were filthy and that he smelled of sweat. Now, she stated that she wouldn't mind him giving her a headsup and not catching her off guard. She said he could've cleaned up his act, but he was inconsiderate.

Conversations

What to talk .... It's not easy to find something to talk to men when they meet up. It's OK to feel nervous. After you meet her at the agreed-upon location, you'll be more relaxed. Let's start with some small talk. "How are things?", "How was your day?" You might also ask how was work. This is to allow you to become more chatty. You can carry on the conversation via text and you can revisit a topic she and you have previously discussed. You can share your day with her, even if it wasn't very exciting. Make it seem exciting. Make sure you know her interests and do some research. Bring them up during the conversation. You should keep up to date with what's happening around the world so that you can share an interesting story. Avoid negative stories.

Please share your funny stories and jokes. If you don't have one, then please share it with someone else. Always be open to asking questions. Talk to her in a stimulating way. Make sure you're interested in her words and her story. This will make you "interesting", whether she is conscious or not. Talkative women tend to be more talkative than men. If this is the case, ask her questions, and then comment on what she is discussing. But even if she isn't very talkative, you should still be talking. Just follow the steps in this section. You can have moments of silence as long it doesn't last for too long. If you are a talkative person, great! Even if the topic isn't of interest to you, speak it anyway! Remember, it's not what your say, but how you say them! If you are passionate about something, it is possible to make it exciting and interesting. Be sure to take her time, listen, and engage in what she says. Ask about the dates she's had with men she met via dating apps. I guarantee she will share her stories with us. Some of the stories that I've heard are just too crazy! Some of the things these men say and do is absolutely hilarious. As you relax, you'll find that you can be more conversational and the conversation flows naturally.

Conclusion

Men are pretty simple creatures, if you want to tell the truth. However, they still have trouble finding what they desire and what makes them happy. A quick Google search will return hundreds of results for women who are all searching the same thing: How do they attract men. There is no one answer. In fact, there are many. Guys are attracted in many ways and it takes multiple factors to be irresistible.

These factors can be found in this book. All you need to learn how to attract men is here. The book is easy to read and understand because it breaks down the information into simple steps, ticks and tips that are easy and straightforward to follow.

Learn how to attract males. You'll also discover why certain male behaviors or preferences exist. This book can be your complete guide to becoming the attractive woman that you've always longed to be.

Just pay attention and make a commitment to becoming every man's dream girl. It's not difficult and any woman can achieve this extraordinary goal if she just puts her mind. It all starts with how you present yourself and ends with your attitude toward the game. This book explains it all for your convenience.